The Château de La Roche-Guyon

Christophe Morin,
architectural historian

Sylvain Hitau,
photographer

Located on a bend in the Seine, the Château de La Roche-Guyon has a unique setting nestled against a steep cliff. From the keep perched on the edge of the Vexin plateau, the view encompasses the valley as far as the villages of Vétheuil, Mantes-la-Jolie, and Saint-Martin-la-Garenne. Standing guard for the king of France in the Middle Ages against the Norman attackers, then the English, the powerful chateau, which was occupied by the German *état-major* during World War II, now braves nothing more than the ravages of time.

During the Renaissance, the Silly family, made counts of La Roche-Guyon, turned the ancient fortress into a country house that welcomed the court during the great hunts. François I, Henri II, and Henri IV liked to stay with the family. After a century and a half, their line died out during the siege of La Rochelle and the estate fell to the Plessis-Liancourt family, also of the nobility, by marriage. In 1659, after another marriage, it passed into the hands of the La Rochefoucauld family, which still owns it. The dukes built the courtyards, vegetable garden, stables, and pavilions during the Enlightenment, while the troglodytic chapels and

Troubadour interiors date from the 19th century. Since 1994, the chateau's management has organised visits, exhibitions, reading, and music rooms.

The lords of La Roche
(12th – 15th century)

The Martyrdom of Saint Nicasius, miniature from *Le Livre d'images de Madame Marie*, folio 79, c. 1255 or 1290 (Paris, BNF, Manuscripts Occ.).

The first mention of the site dates its history back to the 3rd century AD, when Pope Clement I sent Saint Nicasius to evangelise northern Gaul. In the company of Saint Quirinus, he is said to have freed the village of Vaux-sur-Seine from a dragon that threatened its inhabitants. In La Roche-Guyon, on the Rouen road, the pair converted Saint Pience, "noble lady of the place", and Saint Clair, a blind man whose sight they restored. The governor Fescennius, whose jealousy they roused, pursued and martyred them for their Christian faith. According to legend, the grave of Saint Nicasius was hollowed out of the cliff on the site of the chateau's present troglodytic chapel (*Martyrologe*, 1635).

A ghastly hideaway

'Atop a steep promontory above the bank of the great River Seine stands a ghastly and coarse chateau called La Roche; carved out of a high rock, its exterior is invisible. Working the rock, the skilled hand of its builder had created in the slope of the mountain a dwelling of decent size, entered through a small number of mean openings." (Abbot Suger, *Vie de Louis VI* [Life of Louis VI])

This description refers to the primitive housing of the Seine Valley consisting of holes dug in the rock and called *boves*. According to certain authors, this term derives from *bovis* (ox in Latin) and is a reminder that men often lived under the same roof as their livestock. Others think that *bove* comes from the French *boue* (mud), which gave the words *bower* or *bover*— "to dig" in Old French. In any case, there are very few surviving traces of this "dwelling of decent size", which was progressively destroyed as a result of the crumbling of the chalk cliff and during various restorations. It was thought to be located on the site of the present main building and north courtyards of the chateau; the sacristy of the troglodytic chapel is perhaps a vestige of the dwelling.

How Guy, Lord of La Roche, Was Slain by Treachery, miniature from *Les Grandes Chroniques de France de Charles V,* folio 194, c. 1375 – 80 (Paris, BNF, Manuscripts Fr.).

But is it easily understandable that this chateau appeared crude and ominous to Suger, builder of the luminous royal basilica of Saint-Denis and statesman (he was regent of France between 1147 and 1149) always in search of political stability in a country prone to fratricidal wars. During the war over the Vexin region between the king of France and the duke of Normandy, La Roche-Guyon, because of its border location, was a stronghold of the highest strategic importance.

Suger reported that around 1110 Guy de La Roche, the lord of the place and loyal subject of Louis VI le Gros (Louis the Fat), fell under the blows of his father-in-law Guillaume, won over to the Norman cause. The killer and his men of arms executed their victim while he was on his way to mass in the seigniorial chapel. Guy de La Roche was avenged by the king, who regained La Roche-Guyon and moved Guy's descendants back to their seigniory as loyal vassals.

A sturdy stronghold

In 1190 Philippe Auguste granted the lords of
La Roche the privilege of a toll on all merchandise
transported along the Seine between Paris and
Rouen—a toll that was to make their fortune.

It was during the same period that they built the
high tower, an exceptional observatory and place to
watch over river and probably road traffic. The keep
was created at the same time as the fortress built
by Richard the Lionheart, Château Gaillard in the
Eure. Archaeological investigation has determined
three phases in quick succession in the construction
between 1190 and 1200. The tower, built first, had
a remarkable shape: circular by the river, to the south,
and the side open to attack, to the north, featured
a powerful masonry overhang♦, after a system also
used at Issoudun, Indre. The tower's circular section
measures 12 metres in diameter and probably rose
to a height of about 30 metres originally, thus
allowing the surroundings to be watched for miles
around. Its defensive apparatus was subsequently
enriched with a first enceinte, then a second. The
sole access was through an underground staircase
hollowed out of the cliff leading to the troglodytic
dwelling. Directly connected to the seigniorial residence, the tower was nothing more than a three-level
observation post and, was probably never used by
the lords of the manor as a dwelling.

In order to complete this defensive system, the
powerful La Roche dynasty added the two fortified
gates, east and west, to the foot of the cliff during
the first half of the 13th century. With this system,
the lords of La Roche henceforth controlled comings
and goings on the Normandy road that passed

♦**Masonry
overhang:**
pointed man-made
overhang serving as
fortification.

♦**Drop box:**
opening through
which offensive
materials could be
dropped on the
enemy.

♦**Curtain:**
section of wall
connecting two
towers.

Plan of the keep restored by Eugène Viollet-le-Duc, *Dictionnaire raisonné de l'architecture française* (Analytical Dictionary of French Architecture), 1854-68.

...through where the chateau's south main terrace now stands. This type of fortified gate, typical of the era of Philippe Auguste, is at its most sophisticated here: the stonework of the west entrance features two sets of defensive elements separated by a double-door chamber. The visitor had to go under two drop boxes♦, then a portcullis, a double-door chamber, and again through a portcullis in front of the leaves of the door. On the outside, this entrance took on the appearance of two semi-cylindrical towers linked by a curtain♦. To the east, the defence system, few traces of which remain, allowed one to

Fortified east and west gates from the former main building, now part of the present Tour Carrée and Pavillon De Villars.

make one's way to the village upriver or to enter the chateau itself. To the north, there is the same sequence of elements as to the west: portcullis—drop box—drop box—leaves—double-door chamber. This section was probably arranged like that of the west gate, but has now totally disappeared. The south façade—the wall linking the two fortified gates—was greatly transformed during the modern era and is only known through the engravings of Claude Chastillon (see p. 9) and Israël Silvestre (see p. 12). They show that, in the 14th century, the present stable courtyard formed the chateau's outer bailey and accommodated outbuildings constructed against the enceinte wall.

A comfortable manor house

Appointed *grand panetier de France*♦ in 1406, Guy V de La Roche had undertaken considerable work to smarten up his residence and make it more comfortable. The main building, attached to the enceinte's east façade, comprised at that time two rooms in each of the four levels connected by a spiral staircase set in the masonry of the north wall and shielded from potential attackers. Four casement windows brought light into the *bel étage* (first floor), on the south side. On that floor were located, according to a traditional layout that dates back to the Carolingian period, the hall (*aula*), stateroom, and chamber (*camera*), the heart of the apartments of the lords of the manor.

On the second floor, reserved for the more private apartments, the two rooms, which could be modulated with movable partitions or curtains, were lit by four windows, including one on the north façade.

The attic floor featured a similar layout, around the cross wall♦, but the successive alterations of the framework have left few traces of the original layout. Two Renaissance fireplaces give an idea of the prevailing model of the upper floors.

Some unusual elements were signs of extraordinary luxury. From the late 14th century, the groundwater of the Chérence plateau, located over 3 kilometres from the village, was tapped using a network of porous earthenware pipes, then brought by gravitation to the high tower to an underwater reservoir dug halfway up the cliff, then finally to the lower chateau.

The Battle of Agincourt, miniature from *Les Vigiles de Charles VII* by Martial d'Auvergne, folio 11, 1484? (Paris, BNF, Manuscripts Fr.).

The La Roche family also won fame through its interventions in the village. It is to the family that we owe the foundation, in 1087, of a Benedictine priory dedicated to the Holy Trinity, built downstream from the chateau (see pp. 14-15). It was home to a dozen monks with ties to the abbey of Fécamp, who certainly contributed to the installation of water conveyance. The tombs of the lords of La Roche-Guyon, built in the priory chapel, were transferred to the parish church of Saint-Samson in 1780.

The parish church was also another achievement of the La Roche family, who in 1404 obtained the authorisation from Charles VI to demolish the former chateau chapel, located on the site of the main courtyard, in order to replace it with a parish church outside the enceinte. The edifice—finished around 1519—is the last testament to the piety of Guy VI de La Roche, who died at the Battle of Agincourt on 25 October 1415. His widow, Perette de La Rivière, had to withstand alone the English siege led by the Earl of Warwick who, after his victory over the armies of the king of France, had taken Normandy. In 1419 she abandoned her chateau to Guy Le Bouteiller,

♦**Grand panetier de France:** *bread master, officer responsible for the bread at the king's table.*

♦**Cross wall:** *load-bearing wall acting as an internal partition.*

8 | **The chateau c. 1425, discovery of the oldest known depiction** (Free Library of Philadelphia, manuscript Widener 1, f. 61 verso). Jean Mesqui and Claire and Jean Leroy have identified as being located at La Roche-Guyon the six miniatures of *Le Livre du Chastel de Labour*, commissioned by Guy Le Bouteillier and already attributed to the studio of the Bedford Master, or perhaps the Master of Sir John Falstolf. Recognisable are (from top to bottom):
- the double enceinte and the keep tower;
- the cliff before it was extensively hollowed out and the entrance to the underground staircase;
- the main building, with its machicolations and grilled windows, whose west gate, between the bartizan and the corner tower, survives (see p. 5);
- the drawbridge of the closest enceinte (in pink) behind which a terrace already existed;
- the south curtain of the outer bailey and the tower-gate with drawbridge.

♦**Châtelet:** outwork defending a thoroughfare.

whom Henry V of England wanted her to marry, and took refuge with her children at the court of the dauphin, the future Charles VII, at Bourges.
Her son, Guy VII de La Roche, only recovered his estate in 1449. It is likely that he was responsible for the overhaul of the chateau's west façade: in order to reinforce the castle's defences, he built a *châtelet*♦ whose traces are visible under the Terrasse d'Enville, in front of the west gate. During these works, the west gate was raised by one storey, thus increasing the monumentality of the entrance. The last descendant of the lords of La Roche, Guy VII died without a male heir, and the seigniory passed down to his daughter Marie, married first to Michel d'Estouteville and then to Bertin de Silly, Louis XI's chamberlain, to whose descendants fell the fief of La Roche-Guyon.

The times of change
(16th – 18th century)

The Silly dynasty

Enriched by revenues from the octroi, which were supplemented by dues collected on the two fairs founded in 1493 and the salt chamber♦ created by the letter patent of 26 December 1504, the new lords were able to renovate their chateau from top to bottom. In particular, they extended the main building until it joined the west postern. This addition consisted of two rooms on three levels (the building was constructed without a cellar). In order to make the old manor house a pleasant residence, the complex was completed by a wing at a right angle facing

♦*Salt chamber:* *store where one stocked up on salt during the royal monopoly called the "gabelle".*

The Château de La Roche Guion, engraving by Claude Chastillon, *c.* 1600 (AD 95).

west and joining the cliff, where traces of tearing are evidence of the existence of troglodytic rooms to this day. Although there is no existing plan, the engraving by Israël Silvestre leads one to believe that a tower-staircase had been built there to improve the system of getting around.

The chateau had thus become a comfortable courtier's residence, often hosting the court during royal hunts. During one of these visits, the Count of Enghien died in suspicious circumstances. The chronicler Jean de Serres mentions the episode in his *Inventaire de l'Histoire de France* (Inventory of the History of France, 1599):

Renaissance fireplace, chateau attic, late 15th century.

François de Bourbon-Condé (1519–1546)

François de Bourbon, count of Enghien, engraving by Miger after Jean Honoré Fragonard, 19th century (Paris, Bibliothèque de l'Institut).

The fifth son of Charles de Bourbon-Vendôme and Françoise d'Alençon, the Count of Enghien pursued a brilliant diplomatic and military career in northern Italy, theatre of war between France and the imperial armies of Charles V. After emerging victorious at the Battle of Marignano in 1515, then being beaten and taken prisoner at the Battle of Pavia in 1525, François I reopened hostilities in the spring of 1543 by allying himself with Barbarossa. The famous Turkish pirate, whose armada landed at Marseille, was welcomed by François de Bourbon who won a decisive battle against the imperial armies at Ceresole, Piedmont, the following year. This last battle resulted in the peace of Crépy, which marked the end of the Italian Wars. It was thus as a victor that the Count of Enghien arrived at his country home of La Roche-Guyon. His probable murder, followed by those of his brothers, reflected the dynastic tensions in the French court. They ended in the extinction of the Valois dynasty with the assassination of Henri III in 1589 and the accession to the throne of the Bourbons with Henri IV.

The tragic death of François de Bourbon inspired playwright Frédéric Révérend to write a play called *Le Coffre meurtrier* (The Deadly Chest), which is performed at the chateau and has been published by Éditions de l'Amandier in their "La Bibliothèque Fantôme" series (see p. 58).

FRANÇOIS DE BOURBON COMTE D'ENGHIEN

"On 23 February 1546, the snows were great; the court was at La Roche-Guyon. A good many lords who were with the dauphin split into groups to play a game, one to guard a house, the other to assail it with snowballs, but, unfortunately, this pastime soon ended in a fatal accident. As François de Bourbon came out of the house, a chest full of linen, thrown out of the window, fell on his head and in a few days sent him to the grave, not without leaving many suspicions against a few nobles, at that moment jealous of his virtue, reputation, and the favour he had acquired with the king."

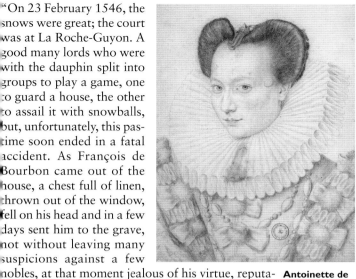

Antoinette de Pons, countess of La Roche-Guyon and then of Plessis-Liancourt, *Portraits dessinés de la Cour de France*, drawing by François Quesnel, c. 1578? (Paris, BNF, Estampes).

François I maintained his confidence in Louis de Silly, however, and his descendants benefited from royal favours. His son Henri (1551 – 1589) was the godson of Henri II and was made count of La Roche-Guyon by Charles IX in 1574. This constant favour led the Silly family to the highest honours as the duchy-peerage♦ of La Roche-Guyon was created in 1621 for François, son of Henri, who was also appointed master of the wolf hunt. This office, which was created by Charlemagne in 812, consisted of organising the eradication of the wolves infesting the provinces. Abolished during the French Revolution, it was replaced in 1805 by the office of the *lieutenant de la louveterie*, who was responsible for the regulation of vermin (boars, foxes, etc.).

François de Silly was mortally wounded in 1628 during the siege of La Rochelle undertaken by Cardinal

♦*Duchy-peerage:* land to which is attached the title of duke and peer of France.

Charles du Plessis, lord of Liancourt, and his wife Antoinette de Pons, white marble sculptures in the round by François Nicolas Guillain for the church of Liancourt, Oise, first quarter of the 17th century (Archives départementales de l'Oise, Mansart de Sagonne coll.).

de Richelieu against the Protestants rebelling against the king. His marriage to Catherine Goyon de Matignon only produced one daughter, who died young. His mother, Antoinette de Pons, in a second marriage to Charles du Plessis-Liancourt gave him a son who held both seigniories, La Roche-Guyon and Liancourt.

The Plessis-Liancourt family

View of the Château de La Rocheguyon in Normandy Belonging to the Lord of Liancourt, engraving by Israël Silvestre, c. 1660 (AD 95).

It was for Roger du Plessis-Liancourt, son of Charles, first gentleman of the king's bedchamber, that Louis XIII transformed the seigniory of La Roche-Guyon into a duchy-peerage in 1643 for the second time. A decade or so later, the new duke started major works to turn the chateau into a vast country house. A first contract, approved in 1652 and kept in the charter room of La Roche-Guyon, details the job of

The main entrance, which used to be to the west of the outer bailey enceinte (see also p. 8, lower right of the miniature, and p. 9, centre of the engraving), was transferred to the east of the main building and replaced by a monumental gate.

re-cutting the cliff on the main courtyard side. The goal of the operation was probably to secure the cliff face and prevent falling rocks but it also aimed to expand the upper courtyard and rationalise the still chaotic appearance of the escarpment. This undertaking was extended to the entire north section, where workers removed several hundred cubic meters of chalk. The rubble thus accumulated was spread in part to produce a vast terrace on the west side of the chateau between 1659 and 1661, and in part to bank up the marshy ground that separated it from the Seine. A new centre of attraction thus rose to the west, leading to the disappearance of the west barbican♦ and its wall.

A gallery-orangery dug out of the foot of the cliff and four windows set in the west wing completed this layout. From the archives, we know that it measured

75 feet long by 18 feet wide and was 17 feet high. Large and pleasant, modern and well positioned, it was at the hospitable heart of the renovated chateau. The 2.7-hectare area newly laid out to the south allowed for the zone to be drained and the new vegetable garden to be designed.

Roger du Plessis-Liancourt married Jeanne de Schomberg in 1620, and the couple lived between the Hôtel de Liancourt in Paris (demolished in 1824 when the rue de l'École-des-Beaux-Arts was built) and their chateaux, La Roche-Guyon and Liancourt, in the Oise. The couple made Liancourt (destroyed during the French Revolution) an enchanting haven where Jeanne de Schomberg attracted a court made up of the most faithful supporters of Port-Royal. Her wisdom and piety were expressed in a book of advice to her granddaughter, *Règlement donné par une dame de haute qualité à M*** sa petite fille, pour sa conduite et pour celle de sa maison…*, which was published after her death in 1698. Indeed, the future of the duchy rested on her granddaughter's shoulders as there were no male heirs.

Jeanne de Schomberg, lady of Plessis-Liancourt, *Portraits dessinés par les Dumoustier,* drawing by Daniel Dumoustier, 1625 (Paris, BNF, Estampes).

The La Rochefoucauld line

The untimely death of Henri Roger de Liancourt, killed during the siege of Mardyck in 1646, had opened the way to new dynastic difficulties and, once again, women played a decisive role in the history of the estate. In 1659 the marriage of Jeanne Charlotte du Plessis-Liancourt, daughter of Henri, to her cousin François VII de La Rochefoucauld meant that it could be kept in the family. Son of the author of *Maxims*, François VII was appointed to the highest offices at court: governor of Berry in 1671, grand master of the king's wardrobe♦ in 1672 and master of the hunt in 1679, his career as a courtier kept him away from the Château de La Roche-Guyon.

With his daughter-in-law, Madeleine Le Tellier, the wife of François VIII de La Rochefoucauld, came a new era of changes. In 1679 the prestigious marriage of the young man to the daughter of Louvois, who succeeded Colbert as Louis XIV's minister of state,

♦**Barbican:** a walled outwork to protect a gate or drawbridge of a fortification.

♦**Grand master of the king's wardrobe:** office created in 1669. The grand master was responsible for the king's clothes and had the privilege of presenting them to him when he arose.

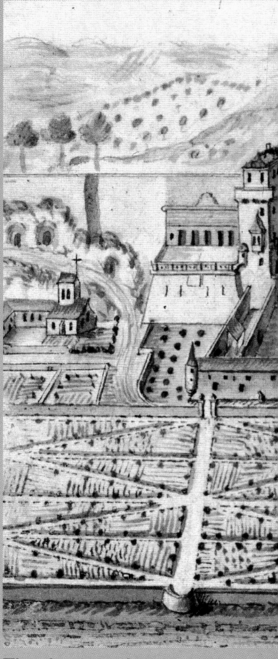

14 | *View of the Château de La Rocheguyon from the Riverbank,* watercoloured drawing, title page of a small handwritten album, 1741 (AD 95).

The chateau reborn

This bird's-eye view shows the large-scale transformations of the modern era: the vegetable garden was formed in the late 17th century and redesigned in 1736 (with the salt chamber in the upper right-hand corner), the upper courtyard—or main courtyard—was reconstructed between 1725 and 1738, and the attic floor topping the main body was added by Duke Alexandre. In 1724 Duchess Madeleine laid out the first spaces for coaches,

visible at the back of the lower courtyard beneath the large south terrace. To the right the fortifications of the east gate, along with the tower and pepperbox turret, were replaced by the De Villars pavilion in 1745. The stable courtyard was still lined with utility buildings, like a fort with its bartizans and *chatêlet* entrance.

This watercolour also shows the appearance of no longer extant buildings, such as the Sainte-Trinité priory (in the plain) and the troglodytic gallery destroyed after 1765 (to the left, on the site of the Pavillon d'Enville).

Monumental portico, main courtyard.

marked the height of royal favour. The Duke of Saint-Simon painted this picture of him:

"He had much honour, worth, and probity. He was noble, good, magnificent, ever willing to serve his friends; a little too much so, for he oftentimes wearied the King with importunities on their behalf. Without any intellect or discernment he was proud to excess, coarse and rough in his manners—disagreeable even…"

(*Memoirs of Louis XIV,*
trans. Bayle St. John, vol. 9, chapter LXIII)

Before long, to maintain the luxurious lifestyle demanded by etiquette, François VIII had to give up his table at the court of Versailles, thus forgoing the services of forty servants, a substantial economy. The strict management of his fortune allowed him to envisage further works at La Roche-Guyon; he decided, with his wife, to plant a large vegetable garden on the banks of the Seine in 1697 and then to transform the main courtyard. On 11 November 1724, the master masons Cauchoix and Olivier signed the following contract:

♦Doric (order): system of architecture characterised by a frieze decorated with metopes (smooth or decorated tablets) and triglyphs (slightly projecting tablets with vertical channels).

♦Ionic (order): system of architecture characterised by capitals decorated with volutes. The Ionic entablature features a smooth, undecorated frieze.

"His Grace ordered the complete demolition of all the buildings that, from the bailey gate on the right-hand side to the wall supporting the former harbour master's office of the chateau, have 84 feet facing towards said courtyard and 132 feet along the battlements. To construct in the same place a uniform building, with a half-attic, of the same length, 18 feet wide on the inside and 27 feet high, that is 8.5 feet for the lower apartments, 9 inches of floor, 7 feet, 9 inches on the first floor and 10 feet of king post."

The document specifies in the margin: "The height of the first floor was decreased to preserve the view from the chateau to the market, which is the reason why the drawing of the second floor had to be removed."

It was, it seems, to build the monumental gate that François VIII called on the services of the young architect Louis De Villars (1711 – 1774). The prestige of such a project undoubtedly demanded the intervention of a professional likely to produce a design whose graciousness matched the owner's ambition. It was a question of transforming the sequence of access to the *bel étage*—and thus to the ceremonial apartments—thanks to a freestone grand staircase on the site of the former rampart. Facing the front, the staircase was to have drawn attention to itself with a triumphal arch adorned with orders of architecture: Doric♦ for the base and colossal Ionic♦ above to support a semicircular arch. Truth to tell, it was unlikely that François VIII was entirely satisfied with the result. The design of the gate, despite the care taken with the proportions and profile of the moulding, looked disordered and awkward. Although the restoration is also partly to blame, this was the work of a novice, particularly the profiles of the architectural ornaments, capitals, and flame finials♦.

In front of the monumental gate, a symmetrical courtyard replaced the various buildings that were located there. An expression of seigniorial power, the regulating layout imposed by the architect is one of great symmetry with at its centre the Pavillon de l'Horloge, covered by a mansard roof♦, in the axis of the church of Saint-Samson and the grand staircase. The entrance to the new main courtyard, featuring a gate flanked by pavilions, echoes the more classical style of the sequence of access to the chateau in the modern era.

The sixth son of François VIII and Madeleine, Alexandre, duke of La Roche-Guyon since his marriage in 1715, had lost five brothers, his two sons, and a daughter when he donned the La Rochefoucauld ducal crown. These many deaths account for the measures he took to secure his estate: by marrying, by pontifical dispensation in 1732, his eldest daughter, Louise Élisabeth, to his nephew, Jean-Baptiste Louis Frédéric de Roye, duke of Enville, and giving them the duchy of

♦**Flame finial:** architectural ornament depicting a vase out of which flames appear to shoot.

♦**Mansard roof:** a roof with a double slope on each of its four sides, allowing for the layout of an attic floor lit by dormer windows. Many 17th-century buildings featured mansard roofs.

Jean-Baptiste de La Rochefoucauld, duke of Enville, print, mid-18th century (Blérancourt, Musée National de la Coopération Franco-Américaine).

The Château de La Roche-Guyon, engraving, 19th century (Paris, BNF, Estampes).

Map of La Roche-Guyon duchy and plan of fountain mains. Watercoloured drawing on parchment, terrier title page, anon., 1745 (AD 95, Charter Room, Château de La Roche-Guyon).

1 Planned orangery
2 Stables

La Roche-Guyon as a wedding present, he guaran-teed the continuity of the duchy-peerage of La Rochefoucauld. Five years later, he married his youngest daughter Marie to Louis François Armand, duke of Estissac—another nephew from the La Rochefoucauld de Roye branch of the family—and gave them the marquisate of Liancourt.

His career as a courtier ended in 1744: the grandson of Jeanne Charlotte du Plessis-Liancourt, known for her devoutness, he did not forgive Louis XV for succumbing once again to the sin of adultery —the king, who was thought to be at death's door in Metz, had let himself be persuaded to make a public confession. Exiled by the king to his estates of La Roche-Guyon and Liancourt, the duke still refused to return to Versailles and devoted all his attention to beautifying his estates.

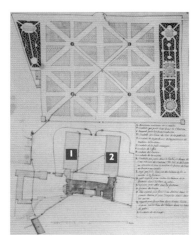

After the main courtyard, he thus decided to refurbish the lower courtyard and commissioned Louis De Villars, his official architect, as well as the sculptor Jamay. In the same spirit as the upper courtyard, the architect proposed a symmetrical plan, flanking the main building with the stables and an orangery as a pendant, as they appear in the *département* archives. For reasons unspecified, only the stables were built. The composition of the group is all the more successful, opening the courtyard to the outside. The development of the approaches revealed the philanthropy of the duke, who, on the occasion of the repairing of the chateau's water mains, had a fountain "for public use" put up. The monument's setting in the village square was a visible sign of his enlightened choices as an aedicule showing that his charity took the place of the traditional image of the gibbet.

A widow at thirty, Louise Élisabeth de La Rochefoucauld, duchess of Enville, helped her father with his works before following in his footsteps. Her friendships with the economist Turgot and Mademoiselle de Lespinasse, her actions alongside Voltaire to clear the name of the Protestant Jean Calas, accused of killing his son, made this devout Catholic one of the most enlightened women of her time. While bringing up her son and daughter she welcomed the Enlightenment elite in her chateau at La Roche-Guyon and her Parisian townhouse in the Faubourg Saint-Germain, putting into practice the principles of physiocracy, an economic doctrine invented in the 18th century by François Quesnay, based on the knowledge and respect of the laws of nature, and with a belief in the supremacy of agriculture.

Between 1765 and 1771, after the disturbances that took place in the chateau's troglodytic gallery, the duchess commissioned from De Villars plans for a new pavil-

Louise Élisabeth de La Rochefoucauld, duchess of Enville, French school, late 18th c. (private coll.).

Anne Robert Jacques Turgot, minister of state, French school, late 18th c. (Château de Versailles).

Louis Alexandre de La Rochefoucauld d'Enville (right) **and cousin François Alexandre de La Rochefoucauld-Liancourt,** English school, late 18th c. (private coll.).

ion to be built to the west of the former dwelling. A veritable paradise within the enceinte of the old chateau, accompanied by a hanging garden opening on to new parterres *à l'anglaise* laid out below, the Pavillon d'Enville was decorated in the *goût moderne*, or taste for the Greek (see p. 52). Tastefully

furnished with gilt wooden chairs designed by Nicolas Heurtaut (1720 – 1771) and upholstered with Gobelins tapestry, the whole was completed by a well-stocked library that contained works on a wide variety of subjects, evidence of the interest taken by the lady of the house and her guests in all fields of knowledge.

Mme d'Enville's **Chateau** by Hubert Robert, oil on canvas, *c.* 1773 – 75 (Rouen, Musée des Beaux-Arts).

Left
Louis Alexandre, Duke of La Rochefoucauld, National Assembly Deputy for Paris in 1789, drawing by J. Guérin engraved by Frantz Gabriel Fiesinger, print, late 18th century (Blérancourt, Musée National de la Coopération Franco-Américaine).

Right
Jean Antoine Nicolas de Caritat, Marquis of Condorcet, oil on canvas, French school, late 18th century (Château de Versailles).

A harsh critic of royal absolutism, Duke Alexandre called for power to be shared between the monarchs and the aristocrats. Like his friend the Marquis of Condorcet (1743 – 1794), his grandson Louis Alexandre thought that the division of society into classes curbed evolution. He advocated a new system of values in which individual merit would replace

The main drawing room of the Duchess of Enville. *Les Anciens Châteaux de France: l'Île-de-France* (Paris, 1924). While the Esther tapestries, commissioned in 1767 from the Manufacture des Gobelins, and the overdoors by Félix Lecomte were returned to their original locations in 2001, the desk known as that "of Louvois" and the seats were broken up in public sales during the late 1980s.

the privilege of birth, and the idea of legal equality filled him with enthusiasm. A close friend of Benjamin Franklin (1706 – 1790), he translated at his request the constitutions of the thirteen American states and hailed the Declaration of Independence, which established freedom of conscience. Elected *député* of the nobility in the States General, he was one of the first to rally the Third Estate and sat with the Parti Patriote in the Constituent Assembly, before becoming president of the provisional municipality of Paris. But on 2 September 1792, he was arrested at Forges-les-Eaux, Eure, on the orders of Jérôme Pétion de Villeneuve (1756 – 1794), mayor of Paris, and killed two days later by rioters at Gisors.

Alexandrine Charlotte de Rohan-Chabot, second wife of Louis Alexandre de La Rochefoucauld, ivory miniature by Louis Lié Périn-Salbreux, c. 1787 (Paris, Musée du Louvre).

The contemporary era (19th – 20th century)

The Viscount of Rohan-Chabot, graphite, red chalk, watercolour, and gouache, drawing by Louis Carrogis, known as Carmontelle, 1760. In 1757 Louis Antoine Auguste de Rohan-Chabot married the daughter of the Duchess of Enville. Their eldest son inherited the chateau after the death of his grandmother (Chantilly, Musée Condé).

Cardinal Louis Auguste de Rohan-Chabot, commemorative statue sculpted by Georges Philippe Clésinger, white marble, 1835. Besançon, cathedral of Saint-Jean (Paris, MAP/AP).

The Rohan-Chabot family

Neither of Louis Alexandre's two marriages produced offspring. The Duchess of Enville ended her days at the Château de La Roche-Guyon with her granddaughter and daughter-in-law, Alexandrine Charlotte de Rohan-Chabot. The chateau thus went to her grandson Alexandre, count of Chabot, duke of Rohan, and prince of Léon, before passing to Alexandre's eldest son, Louis François Auguste.

The seigniory of La Roche-Guyon thus passed out of the hands of the La Rochefoucauld family for 37 years. Turning to religion after the tragic death of his wife, the great-grandson of the Duchess of Enville injected new life into

The church of Saint-Samson, postcard, c. 1910. *The Adoration of the Magi* hung above the high altar has been attributed to the painter Giuseppe Bartolomeo Chiari. It was given to the church in 1803 by the Duchess of Rohan, princess of Léon, whose son was ordained a priest in La Roche-Guyon in 1822.

the old residence for a decade. The works he undertook focussed mainly on the chapels, built from 1816-18. Ordained to the priesthood in La Roche-Guyon in 1822, he hosted the most brilliant clergymen in France, such as Father Dupanloup, bishop of Orléans, Abbot of Héricourt, the future bishop of Autun, and Prince Jules de Polignac, minister to Charles X. Alphonse de Lamartine spent Holy Week there in 1819, and wrote one of his *Méditations poétiques*. Victor Hugo, whom he met the same year at the seminary of Saint-Sulpice, came to La Roche-Guyon in 1821 and again in 1835. Appointed archbishop of Besançon in 1829, the prince-cardinal sold the estate of the eldest son of François Alexandre Frédéric de La Rochefoucauld-Liancourt. This second grandson of Duke Alexandre on his mother's side, had, after his return from exile, obtained all the titles of his relations who died during the French Revolution.

The troglodytic chapels, lithograph by Adolphe Maugendre, c. 1850 (AD 95, Charter Room, Château de La Roche-Guyon).

Warehouses at La Roche-Guyon, engraving, 19th century (Paris, BNF, Estampes).

The La Rochefoucauld family

In the early 19th century, the port, which had made the fortune of the lords of the manor and of the village, still sold stones hauled from the quarry of Chérence and sheets of zinc produced by the rolling mills of Bray-et-Lû. It went rapidly into decline after the construction of the railway in the Epte river valley but the growth of tourism to the landscapes of the banks of the Seine saved the village, where the number of inns multiplied. The bend in the river, the rugged hills, the mean troglodytic dwellings, Madame d'Enville's landscaped garden, and the old tower in ruins all became subjects sought out by artists and lithographers. Around 1850, Adolphe Maugendre engraved an entire book of plates depicting the village and its chateau for the publisher Adolphe Bry

Troglodytic dwellings at La Roche-Guyon, lithograph by Édouard Holstein, 1843 (Paris, BNF, Estampes).

and, in 1854, the architect Eugène Viollet-le-Duc published the first archaeological survey of the keep. His hosts, converts to the Troubadour style, had the dining room and the guardroom decorated in neo-Renaissance style. Painted on the inner shutters, the arms of the various branches of the La Rochefoucauld line proclaimed the age of the family.

The village modernised. A new town hall and more comfortable houses replaced the old market, dwellings, and cemetery. Since 1838, a suspension bridge has made crossing the river easy. In the mid-19th century, the youngest son of Duke François XIV de La Rochefoucauld, Count Georges (1821 – 1861), persuaded his father to have a guardhouse built in a small enclosure to house convalescent children from Paris hospitals.

Romantic views of La Roche-Guyon, lithographs, mid-19th century (Paris, BNF, Estampes).

The guardroom.

Taking up a tradition begun by Hubert Robert in the 18th century and attracted to the picturesque location, the Impressionists who worked in the Oise and Seine river valleys liked to paint from life. Camille Pissarro produced a drypoint of the

The guardroom, *Les Anciens Châteaux de France: l'Île-de-France* (Paris, 1924).

Château de La Roche-Guyon in 1880. One year later, Claude Monet, who had just left Vétheuil for Giverny, painted *The Seine between Vétheuil and the Château de La Roche-Guyon*. In 1885 Auguste Renoir depicted the grocer's shop where he stayed in *Landscape at*

Ceiling, dining room.

The son of the stars

The youngest son of Duke Pierre and Duchess Isabelle de La Rochefoucauld was keen on esotericism. Count Marie Joseph Auguste Antoine (1862–1959) was, in the late 19th century, grand prior of the Ordre de la Rose-Croix Catholique, du Temple et du Graal. He financed the ten issues of the illustrated monthly *Le Coeur*, which blended esotericism, literature, science, and art and was published from 1893-95 and organised several Rosicrucian expositions at the Durand-Ruel gallery in which Camille Pissarro and his sons, Émile Bernard, or Paul Signac took part.

The Young Nabi
by Antoine de
La Rochefoucauld,
oil on canvas,
signed and dated
1893 (Château de
La Roche-Guyon,
Cg 95 AOA).

♦*Rosicrucianism:*
Hermetist order
closely related to
the Masonic
movements of the
Enlightenment.
It experienced a
revival influenced
by Joséphin Péladan
(1858-1918),
who inspired
the symbolist
movement.
This writer styled
himself "Sâr"
(prophet king)
or "Magus".

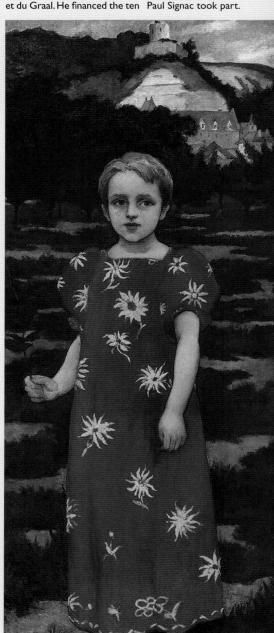

Landscape at La Roche-Guyon by Auguste Renoir, 1885 (Aberdeen, Art Gallery).

La Roche-Guyon. Émile Zola and Paul Cézanne left Paris on the first Sunday train and got off at Bonnières station. "It was quite a business. Paul took a panoply of painter's gear. As for me, I just had a book in my pocket," wrote Zola, who fished, swam, and took notes for his future novel *L'Œuvre* (*The Masterpiece*); during this period, his friend tried to depict "superb things", and came up with a new way of looking at landscape by combining different picture planes in his *Winding Road at La Roche-Guyon*, which was left unfinished. Also in 1909, Georges Braque spent the summer deconstructing the chateau in nine cubist views. Only one can be seen in French public collections, in the Musée d'Art Moderne of Villeneuve-d'Ascq.

The Château de La Roche-Guyon, wood and cork model by the chateau's manager, Hippolyte Alexandre (1763 – 1843), before the removal of the main building's attic floor (Château de La Roche-Guyon, Cg 95 AOA).

1 Landscaped garden waterfall (see p. 61)
2 Reservoir terrace

The stables and the Tour Carrée after the bombings of August 1944, photograph by Emmanuel Mas (Paris, MAP/AP).

♦**Attic:**
a space or room within the roof of a house. Also a low wall or storey above the entablature of a classical façade.

Twenty years earlier, in order to hark back to the "Renaissance" look of the chateau, its proprietors got rid of the attic♦ floor that the Duchess of Enville had built where the roof space used to be. Only the model kept in the stables, and a few traces in the loft, remind us that the chateau thus saw its surface area increased by a third in order to house the duchess's many servants.

In the first half of the 20th century, no major changes were made to the chateau but it was greatly damaged during World War II. On 9 June 1940, the dynamiting of the bridge by the French Engineers to slow the advance of the Wehrmacht shattered the windows. On 27 August 1944, during the French campaign, eight Allied bombs destroyed the outbuildings of the upper courtyard, leaving the attic of the

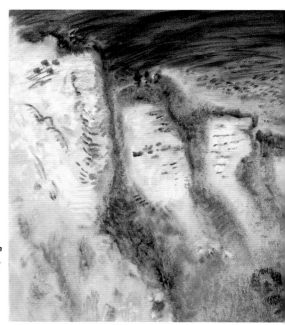

The Seine at La Roche-Guyon by André Masson, 1952 (Paris, Musée National d'Art Moderne, Centre Georges Pompidou).

main building wide open. Thanks to its listing as a historic monument in 1943, the programmes overseen by the Monuments Historiques chief architect allowed all the buildings to be restored. The salvage campaign continued until 1963.

In 1987 the chateau's collection was broken up at auctions in Monaco and Rouen. The combined efforts of the French government, the Conseil Général du Val-d'Oise, and the Association pour la Sauvegarde et l'Animation Culturelle de La Roche-Guyon allowed for a part of the site to be opened. Since 2003, it has been run by a public institution for cultural cooperation.

The post-war years.
The restoration of the Tour Carrée, equipped with a roof terrace, is finished, that of the main courtyard is in progress but the outbuildings have not yet been covered. The vegetable garden is still in use. Photograph by Roger Henrard, c. 1955 (AD 95).

Visit

evel 0

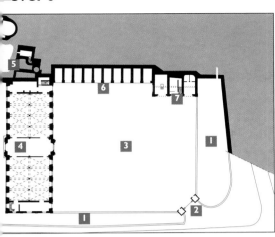

1 Moat
2 Gate
3 Lower courtyard or stable courtyard
4 Stables
5 Foundations of the Tour Carrée
6 Coach house
7 Pavillon de Villars (ground floor)

The vegetable garden

The works undertaken by Roger du Plessis-Liancourt in 1652 helped drain the land that separated the chateau from the Seine, thanks to an embankment resulting from the cutting of the cliff. The only garden on the estate until the creation of the landscaped garden paths of the hill, the vast 2.7-hectares space was redesigned beginning in 1736 by Duke Alexandre de La Rochefoucauld's landscape architect. It comprises four square plots with round basins in their centres, around which are arranged triangular beds. An invaluable inventory from 1741 has allowed the beds to be recreated as they were during the Enlightenment: 442 pear trees, 143 apple trees, 74 peach trees, and 16 plum trees, including 2 exotic species. It demonstrates the duke's interests in the sciences, and botany in particular, like other great physiocrat nobles concerned with improving the yields of land under cultivation. Fertile ground for experimentation, the garden was also an agreeable place, as evidenced by the copses with winding paths recreated on a strip of land to the west of the vegetable garden and on a triangular parcel to the southeast. In the northeast corner of the vegetable garden, a small building sheltered La Roche-Guyon's salt chamber in the 18th century.

The vegetable garden seen from the keep.

The lower courtyard, or stable courtyard

The stable courtyard appears today as it did when Duke Alexandre and his architect Louis De Villars refitted it out from 1740. Opposite the metal gate topped with the La Rochefoucauld arms —a masterpiece of rocaille ironwork by the ironsmith Le Tellier put in place around 1745—the stable building is punctuated by ten bays distributed around a monumental central gate. It is likely that stability problems forced De Villars to replace the coach house

commissioned by Duchess Madeleine Le Tellier in 1725 at the foot of the terrace (depicted on the title page of the vegetable garden inventory, see pp. 14-15). On this occasion, the architect used elements of the stable arcade for the elevation of the coach house as well as the first bay of the pavilion that bears his name today in order to harmonise the whole of the courtyard. The destruction of the enceinte walls still visible in the late 17th century to make room for the dry ditches

llowed the public to see
he symmetrical architecture
of the courtyard.
The ditches, planted with rows
of lime trees until
he mid-20th century, have
ince been sown with grass.

The coach house

On the keystones of the coach
house are numbered metal
plaques, which allowed the
host to ask for his coach and
horses from the groom.

Rearing horse on the stable pediment, sculpture by Jamay, c. 1745.

The stables

Of the sober project of Louis De Villars, which consisted of framing the main building with two symmetrical buildings, an orangery and a stable, only the later was built. The architect demonstrated a perfect knowledge of the latest fashions in equestrian architecture.

The avant-corps of the stables offers a harmonious synthesis of the most recent major monuments.

The large archivolt♦ of the gate, supported by Doric rusticated♦ pilasters♦, is reminiscent of that built by Jean Aubert for the dome of the stables of Chantilly (1720), while the tympanum♦ explicitly refers to the horses that Guillaume I Coustou was completing for Marly (1745) but whose plaster models he had been exhibiting in his studio since 1740.

♦**Archivolt:** ornamental moulding around the top of an arch.

♦**Rustication:** masonry consisting of large cut stone blocks that are smooth or roughly hewn.

♦**Pilaster:** a shallow column attached to the face of a wall.

♦**Tympanum:** the space between the lintel and the arch situated above it.

Inside, the stable consists of two large rooms on either side of a through hallway adorned with Doric corner pilasters echoing those of the façade.

Here again, the reference to Chantilly is still clear, although less ostentatiously luxurious. It is unlikely, however, that this room was used as an indoor riding school as it was too small for riding lessons to be held in it. On either side, rib-vaulted stables feature a mixed brick-and-stone dressing reminiscent of that used by Jules Hardouin-Mansart at Versailles.

The original layout of the boxes around mid-height longitudinal walls is explained by the large openings.

They are at variance with the darkness that should usually reign over this type of building in order to calm the horses. Seriously damaged by the Allied bombings of 27 August 1944, the stables were not restored until 1956 by George Lisch, chief architect of the Monuments Historiques.

This horse held back by a groom belongs to a group known as the "Horses of Marly" sculpted by Guillaume Coustou I for the basin of the Château de Marly's watering place, Carrara marble, 1740 – 45 (Paris, Musée du Louvre).

Stables, interior, exhibition by François Hilsum, 2007.

The Pavillon De Villars

The imposing square pavilion with three bays on six levels, built between 1765 and 1771 by Louis De Villars, replaced the medieval *châtelet*. In the past, the space was multifunctional. There were sheds and storerooms on the ground floor, the servants' accommodation was located on the first mezzanine, and the chateau charter room was on the second mezzanine; comfortable guestrooms were spread out over the three remaining floors.

The first three levels, visible from the front under moulded arches, feature a vaulted head that contributes to the buttress of the main building. The dogleg stair serving the mezzanines is also cradle-vaulted.

As for the square floors, they are served by a huge staircase that is accessible from the chateau's entrance hall. The Pavillon De Villars is now home to the offices of the Établissement Public du Château de La Roche-Guyon.

The Pavillon De Villars staircase leads to the main terrace located above the coach house.

Level 1

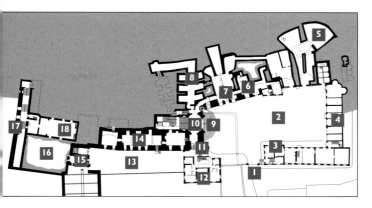

The main south terrace and the Tour Carrée

From the Pavillon De Villars, you can reach the main terrace located above the coach house in the stable courtyard. The terrace corresponds to the medieval road that went past the chateau's south façade. On this level, the loopholes connecting the cellars of the medieval dwelling were replaced, during the time of the Liancourt family, by windows meant to bring light into the kitchens. Edged by a stone balustrade built around 1745, the terrace, adorned with flowerbeds, leads to the square tower. Built by the Silly family, it encompasses the fortified west gate, which in the past was flanked by two semicircular towers, whose interior is still in place. The layout of the defence system, typical of the era of Philippe Auguste, was organised around a double-door chamber, preceded by two drop boxes and a portcullis, then a second portcullis and leaves.

1 Gate
2 Upper courtyard
3 *Auditoire* and prison
4 Pavillon de l'Horloge
5 *Boves*
6 Modern kitchens
7 Orangery
8 Pillboxes
9 Monumental portico
10 Main staircase
11 East gate
12 Pavillon De Villars
13 South main terrace
14 Main building (medieval kitchens)
15 West gate
16 Terrasse d'Enville
17 Theatre staircase
18 Theatre

The upper courtyard and the outbuildings

During the Middle Ages, the upper courtyard was occupied by the chateau chapel, which was replaced after 1404 by the parish church outside the enceinte. Until it was transformed into a courtyard around 1725, it took the shape of a square delineated by two wings clinging to the cliff. It became part of the longitudinal axis of the main building, centred on a pavilion whose slate-covered square roof was topped by a roof light

Upper courtyard entrance gate, detail.

The Time Trap

In 1960 Edgar Pierre Jacobs published the ninth volume in the comic book series of adventures of Blake and Mortimer. In *Le Piège diabolique* (*The Time Trap*), the author recounts the adventures of his hero, Professor Philip Mortimer, at La Roche-Guyon. Jacobs immersed himself in the Château de La Roche-Guyon thanks to photos taken there, the tiniest details of which we find in the comic book. Throughout the book appear the lanes of the village, the keep, and the *boves*. One of the *boves* (housing the orangery) contains the chronoscaph, a diabolical time machine invented by the mad Dr. Miloch, Mortimer's adversary, in the previous album *S.O.S. Meteors*.

The famous chronoscaph reconstructed in one of the boves.

By Jove ! le décor est digne de la légende !...

Illustration from the comic book *The Time Trap,* devoted to the adventures of Blake & Mortimer.

that echoes the bell tower of Saint-Samson: thus, from the "Chambre du Cardinal", the clergy and the nobility of the *ancien régime* are visually linked.

The main courtyard is entered through a gate put up in 1786, flanked by a pavilion whose twin was taken down in the late 18th century.

The surviving pavilion now houses the chateau's visitor reception area. Before the French Revolution, it was occupied by the *auditoire seigneurial*♦, which was next to the prison; the presence of these public services in the main courtyard proceeded from the staging of nobiliary prerogatives.

There was accommodation on two levels for the servants, then spaces for coaches in the main building at a right angle. Opposite the *auditoire*, the north wing is attached to a pavilion that itself is partially troglodytic.

In the *boves*, there remain a bread oven, several sheds, and an orangery with French windows framed by two windows under a masonry avant-corps.

♦**Auditoire seigneurial:** *room in which a lord rendered justice.*

The pillboxes

The setting up of a German civil air defence post at the Château de La Roche-Guyon, beginning in August 1943, left unexpected traces. In order to protect a large supply of ammunition, huge tunnels were dug out of the cliff by Polish prisoners to the north of the main staircase.

These pillboxes consist of twelve square cells organised around a long sloping U-shaped corridor. Their entrance is commanded by an explosion-proof wall, which is still visible, made out of high-density concrete.

The exhibition displayed in the pillboxes goes back over the principal events of World War II as seen from La Roche-Guyon.

On 9 July 1940, to slow down the Wehrmacht's advance, the French army blew up the bridge built by engineer Nicolas Esquillan (1902 – 1989) and inaugurated in July 1935. The German troops that occupied the village in August 1940 took over the chateau in 1943 to set up a civil air defence post there. Field Marshal Erwin Rommel (1891 – 1944), put in charge of the Atlantic Wall, which was built to prevent the Allied landings, set up his *état-major* at La Roche-Guyon in February 1944.

The writer Ernst Jünger (1895 – 1998), then a military attaché, dedicated some fine pages to the site in his war diary. A week after the departure of the Germans in August 1944, the Allies bombed the village and the chateau, seriously damaging its roofing.

The buildings' listing as historical monuments in 1943 meant that major restorations could be financed; these came to an end with the restoration of the Pavillon De Villars in 1963.

Level 2

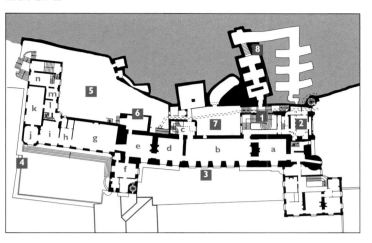

The chateau entrance, the main staircase

The chateau entrance, designed by Louis De Villars, is an opening in the 14th-century rampart, as the round tower that flanks it to the left attests. Its pendant, built against the cliff, houses a spiral staircase leading to the gangway encircling the façade and leading to an astronomical observatory that Louis Alexandre de La Rochefoucauld had built at the top of the south turret. The entrance portico comprises two floors linked by a colossal Ionic order. On the ground floor, Doric pilasters flank a large formerly frameless window. On the first floor, French windows open on to a balustrade framed by flame finials, while the roundheaded window of the second floor, accentuated by a monumental archivolt, commands the entrance to an ironwork balcony. Ionic pilasters and columns give this composition depth, but the uncertain design of this façade betrays the hand of an inexperienced architect. The lack of a clear choice between the medieval aesthetic and the *goût moderne*

1 Main staircase
2 Chambre du Cardinal
3 Main building
a Dining room
b Salle des Gardes
c Red staircase
d Billiard room
e Petit salon
f Cabinet de la Tour Carrée
4 Pavillon d'Enville
g Salon de Madame d'Enville
h Antichambre de la Duchesse
i Chambre de la Duchesse
j Salon d'Angle
k Library
l Cabinet des Curiosités
m Cabinet des Portraits
n Entrance hall
5 Cour des Chiens
6 Laboratory
7 Cour des Cerfs
8 Pillboxes

Main staircase,
Les Anciens Châteaux de France: l'Île-de-France
(Paris, 1924).

The façade on the main courtyard with its monumental portico.

Detail of stained glass of the main staircase.

is particularly evident in the upper sections where the architect has kept the 14th-century parapet walk but has transformed the machicolation♦ into a rather unusual cyma♦.

De Villars proved to be more at ease with issues of distribution. Thus, the ingenious placing of the main staircase on the longitudinal axis of the main building confers majesty on the entrance to the ceremonial apartments.

On the ground floor, the wide staircase leads to an entrance hall from which the east gate may be reached by a double-door chamber. In the 13th century, it comprised a sequence of leaves, two sets of drop boxes, and a portcullis. The first flight of stairs, edged with a stone balustrade, led to an intermediate landing lit by two large windows decorated with the La Rochefoucauld arms in stained glass. The effect of domination thus produced reminds the visitor of the rank of the lord of the manor. The landing connects to the Salle des Gardes (guardroom) and, via a wooden return in imitation of stone, leads to the room known as the "Chambre du Cardinal", whose woodwork dates from 1733. This room has wonderful views of the main courtyard and the church of Saint-Samson.

The Salle des Gardes

Though decorated in the 1880s, the Salle des Gardes (guardroom) still looks the way it did when this part of the main building was constructed in the 14th century. This is where the main episodes of the public life of the lords of La Roche and their successors took place. On the room's south side are five windows that were enlarged in the 17th century; their embrasures bear the coats of arms of the principal members of the La Rochefoucauld family. The leaves of the doors are decorated with military trophies in an eclectic style inspired by the reign of Louis XIV, as was the coffered ceiling where the initials of the La Rochefoucauld family and their motto, "*C'est mon plaisir*" (It's my pleasure), alternate. The niche near the room's entrance was equipped with a faience stove in the past, which probably replaced a monumental fireplace similar to that of the attic (see p. 9). The floor in hard limestone with slate accents is a legacy of the 18th-century restorations.

♦Machicolation: *overhanging opening for the launching of projectiles.*

♦Cyma: *a double-curved moulding.*

The dining room

This room was the bedchamber of the lords of the manor in the Middle Ages. Belatedly transformed into a dining room, in the late 19th century it was decorated in the neo-Renaissance style and was equipped with a service lift hidden in the wainscoting. Access to the first floor of the Pavillon De Villars is through a small lodge fitted out above the double-door chamber of the medieval gate.

The "Chambre du Cardinal"

♦*Pier:*
part of a wall between two windows. Above a fireplace, panel often adorned with a mirror.

This is one of the most important rooms in the chateau. It opens on to the main courtyard by French windows under the monumental triumphal arch of the main staircase and demonstrates the strong presence of the duke and all his prerogatives: it towers above the *auditoire*, prison, and coach house punctuated by arches and covered by a mansard roof in the axis of the bell tower of the parish church,

the final resting place
of his ancestors.
The polychromy of the
tile-and-slate roof (the latter
material, more noble, was only
used for the central pavilion)
adds to the spectacular staging
of seigneurial privileges.
Lovely rocaille woodwork
decorated the walls of the
room, forming an alcove
equipped with a fireplace
with pier♦.
The woodwork was executed
during the restoration of the
interiors under taken in 1720
– 30 by Duke François VIII de
La Rochefoucauld and his
wife Madeleine.

The billiard room

The creation of the billiard room dates back to the second stage of construction of the main building, as shown by the damaged coat of arms of the Silly family above the fireplace. The wainscoting and the mantelpiece were added to the room in the late 17th century. The faience stove is evidence of the comfort

Damaged Silly coat of arms.

sought by Enlightenment society in this room dedicated to games. On the wall is a large terrier map drawn in 1737 showing the extent of the duchy of La Roche-Guyon. The disadvantages of the series of linked rooms in a main building that is one-room deep meant that it had to be made two-rooms deep in places in order to facilitate getting around. That is why in the 18th century, a staircase known as the "red staircase" was put in on the north façade behind the Salle des Gardes and billiard room. It leads to the private apartments of the second floor, where the bedchamber known as that of Henri IV was once located.

The Petit Salon and the tower cabinets

The Petit Salon, adjacent to the billiard room, occupies a central place in the layout of the ceremonial apartments. In the 17th century, it commanded the north entrance of the library wing and of the troglodytic gallery dug during the time of Roger du Plessis-Liancourt. After the Duchess of Enville had removed these elements, a small lean-to building was added to the main building. Now blocked up, it once housed the laboratory of Louis Alexandre de La Rochefoucauld. The Petit Salon's elegant rocaille woodwork decor dates to the 1730s, the period when Duchess Madeleine endeavoured to modernise the chateau. To the south, a door opens on to a cabinet and a back-cabinet in the Tour Carrée that offer particularly

interesting views of the terraces and the stable courtyard. The modest size of these spaces takes us back to the private sphere of the lords of La Roche-Guyon. Outside the main series of linked rooms, the cabinet was a luxurious retreat that was wainscoted and decorated with mirrors.

Play of light, cabinet in the Tour Carrée.

Rocaille decor, Petit Salon.

The Pavillon d'Enville, south façade, behind the Tour Carrée.

The Pavillon d'Enville

When in 1765 the ceiling of the troglodytic gallery showed alarming signs of weakness, Madame d'Enville decided to reconstruct a pavilion in the centre of the chateau's west terrace, which was built between 1659 and 1661, above the medieval barbican. The building's complex programme, which meets the utmost modern standards of comfort in a magnificent decor, comprised a theatre in the basement, a ceremonial apartment on the ground floor, and private rooms on the first floor.

The magical nature of this wing is reinforced on the one hand by the presence of a hanging garden, on the same level as the main drawing room, and on the other by its location at the westernmost end of the chateau.

In the perpendicular wing, the windows look out on the landscaped garden below. The duchess's guests thus covered 80 metres from the main courtyard before arriving at the Pavillon d'Enville. This distancing characterised the aristocratic aesthetic of chateau layouts. It brings to mind the incredible journey that Louis XIV had the ambassador of Siam make during his 1686 visit—through the courtyard and then the hall of mirrors at the end of which stood the throne.

Sundial, terrace of the Pavillon d'Enville.

The Salon de Madame d'Enville

The imposing drawing room of 130 square metres combines luxurious materials with refined decor. It is one of finest works by Louis De Villars and demonstrates how he perfectly assimilated carved by Félix Lecomte (1737 – 1817), the official sculptor of Claude Nicolas Ledoux. They depict the allegory of Fortune (to the west), under whose influence prospers the Spirit of the Arts (to the east).

The Spirit of the Arts, marble bas-relief by Félix Lecomte, 1769.

the new taste for the Greek. The drawing room was lit by three French windows that opened on to the hanging garden. Twelve pearl grey and white Corinthian pilasters punctuate the walls, framing doors, windows, fireplace, and tapestries. They support an entablature decorated with modillions♦ and egg patterns, a more ornate version of the Corinthian order. Around the doors, fasces tied up with ribbons link the windows to exquisite bas-relief overdoors

This flattering metaphor is a reminder of the patronage of the La Rochefoucauld family, underlined by the plan of the Pavillon d'Enville held by one of the putti accompanying the Spirit of the Arts. The room's decor was completed by remarkable gilt wood furniture by Nicolas Heurtaut (1720 – 1771): twelve armchairs and two sofas upholstered in Gobelins tapestries with a multicoloured flower pattern on a pink ground, which were sold in 1987.

♦Modillion:
series of small brackets placed underneath a cornice.

Sale and return of the furniture

This sofa is one of the drawing room's seats designed by Nicolas Heurtaut in 1769. The group is today partly in public collections (notably the Musée du Louvre) and partly in private ones (private coll.).

The furniture in Madame d'Enville's drawing room was sold in 1987.

Only the Esther tapestries returned to the chateau in 2001.

The Esther tapestries

The Book of Esther tells how Mordecai, leader of the Jewish Diaspora in Persia, persuaded his niece to marry King Ahasuerus (Xerxes I, 485–465 BC) and how the young woman saved her people by foiling the plots of the grand vizier Haman.

In 1689, at the request of Madame de Maintenon, Racine wrote the tragedy Esther for the convent girls at Saint-Cyr. From 1737 to 1742, first painter to the king Jean-François de Troy designed an Esther tapestry in seven cartoons for the Manufacture des Gobelins. In 1767 Madame d'Enville kept four of the tapestries to decorate her main drawing room: the first two illustrate Esther's preparations before meeting the king and the complete success of her undertaking; in the third, Mordecai (standing right) refuses to bow before the grand vizier; in the last, the wrathful king (standing right) subjects his minister (standing left) to public obloquy.

*The Toilet,
The Crowning,
**The Disdain of
Mordecai,**
and **The
Condemnation
of Haman*** were bought back for the chateau by the Conseil Général du Val-d'Oise. Workshops of Audran and Cozette, 1768–69 (Cg 95 AOA).

The Antichambre de la Duchesse

This small wallpapered room is the first in the apartments used by Duchess of Enville for socialising. It is one of the rare surviving examples of this type of decor still *in situ*.

The 18th century had a fondness for all that was exotic, a synonym for luxury and modernity. The furnishings were recreated using pieces from the neighbouring Château de Villarceaux.

To the north, it communicates with two wardrobes, one of which could be used as a bathroom.

The Chambre de la Duchesse or Chambre de Zénaïde

This ceremonial room's decor features wainscoting and two facing mirrors whose frames are decorated with finely sculpted garlands of flowers and vases.

The furniture comprises a "pulpit" bed, a pair of folding screens embroidered with flowers, and a few 18th-century chairs.

The bedchamber was named after Duchess Zénaïde de La Rochefoucauld (1798 – 1875), née Chapt de Rastignac.

The Salon d'Angle

This room is the hinge between the east-west axis and the north-south axis of the Pavillon d'Enville. Its most attractive feature is this double aspect.

The library

The library constitutes, along with the d'Enville drawing room, the major room of the new pavilion and the star attraction of its apartments. It housed nearly 10,000 volumes before they were sold in 1987. The dummies that replace them poetically evoke these lost splendours. Only a few books arranged in a display case in the centre of the room, the gifts of Julien Lacaze, jurist and patron, are reminders of the great variety of subjects

Library book (AD 95).

Title page of a book from the library.

Le Coffre meurtrier **(The Deadly Chest)**, a volume in the Bibliothèque Fantôme collection created by the chateau. The series also includes another play, *13 semaines de vertu* (13 Weeks of Virtue), which tells of the strange discipline that Benjamin Franklin imposed upon himself, and historical works like *Franklin des deux mondes* (Franklin of the Two Worlds) by Daniel Vaugelade.

broached in the library where the Duchess of Enville collected the works of her physiocrat friends in particular. Located behind the library, a small room makes the transition with the corridor that leads to the Cour des Chiens. The recreations exhibited in the display cases evoke a modest cabinet of curiosities—a far cry from the magnificent collections put together by Madame d'Enville and her son in their Parisian townhouse in the Faubourg Saint-Germain.

In the next cabinet, eight portraits engraved on steel present the different fates of members of the La Rochefoucauld family during the French Revolution.

The entrance hall of the Pavillon d'Enville

Corridor leading to the theatre and graffiti.

On display here are the models of the small theatre built by the Duchess of Enville under the terrace and now inaccessible. It was reached through a very long monumental corridor with windows overlooking the landscaped garden to the south.

The landscaped garden, closed for safety reasons, may be visited by appointment only.

Previous page
Landscaped garden behind the stables.

The Pavillon d'Enville, west façade on the landscaped garden.

Grotto in the landscaped garden.

The gardens of La Roche-Guyon

The absence of a pleasure garden surrounding the Château de La Roche-Guyon before the second half of the 18th century—with the exception of the vegetable garden—is explained by the unusual layout of the main building, wedged between the cliff and the river. The intervention of the Duchess of Enville, who proceeded little by little, shows how difficult it was for her to make coherent the area surrounding her estate. In 1764 she had an esplanade of about 3 hectares planted slightly downstream from the chateau, on a part of the Île aux Boeufs that had up until that point been used only for pasture. Then, following the fashion of her time, she decided in 1769 to plant an irregular garden south of the new pavilion, behind the stables: from the Terrasse d'Enville, visitors could thus enjoy the copses of greenery and winding paths of the new space. After this project, the duchess organised a network of regular avenues providing a shady promenade to the Île aux Boeufs. The group of gardens at the foot of the chateau was supplemented in 1787 with an open-air ballroom (on the site of the present car park) that was put at the disposal of the villagers, as Madame d'Enville was in favour of the new ideas of Turgot and Rousseau. Madame du Deffand wrote this about the duchess: "This woman is completely besotted with modern

Route of an old pathway and waterfall in the landscaped garden.

physiocracy, but she practices it more than she preaches it."

The duchess's master plan began to take shape in 1777. It consisted of linking all the estate's gardens and the keep. The following year, this ambition materialised with the building of a door framed with a Doric portico in the enceinte of the old tower (see p. 66). The keep, integrated into the network of the grounds' ornamental buildings, thus became a sublime belvedere from which a walker could see the whole valley. The architect Prepsac and the engineer of the *généralité* of Paris, Didier Ulriot de Montfeu, opened up paths on the hillside as they appear on the watercolour of Louis de Lespinasse. These major works, both in terms of earthworks and of planting, ground to a halt because of the revolutionary unrest in 1791. The chateau gardens were filled with ornamental buildings, particularly six "cool rooms" hollowed out of the cliff, decorated with rockwork and furnished with benches especially designed for them. Another pavilion in the shape of a thatched cottage was placed on the top of the promenade. But the most spectacular addition was undoubtedly the large waterfall installed northwest of the chateau, whose complex hydraulic network could, thanks to two reservoirs, produce the picturesque effects of a cataract over 30 metres high.

The Cour des Cerfs and Cour des Chiens

**The Cour
des Cerfs.**

The shape of these two courtyards changed markedly over the centuries.
The hollowing out of the cliff, the construction of the wing joining the chateau to the troglodytic gallery in the 17th century, and then its destruction in 1774 in the Cour des Chiens and the destruction of the spiral staircase replaced by the "red staircase" and the main staircase in the 18th century in the Cour des Cerfs, have made these spaces rich in archaeological vestiges difficult to decipher.

The view of them from the parapet walk or the Galerie des Chapelles shows the overlapping of the valleys, whose assembly is stunning to look at.
The various parts of the roof were covered in slate or wood shingles.
During recent restorations, wood shingles were preferred for the sections most at risk from falling rocks because of their shock resistance.

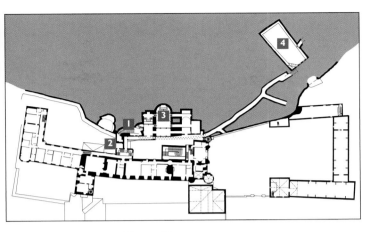

The Galerie des Chapelles and the chapels

The picturesque entrance to the series of troglodytic chapels refurbished by Cardinal Louis François Auguste de Rohan is through a narrow timber-framed corridor, looking out over the Cour des Chiens through small roundheaded windows. The fragments of sculpture, embedded in the gallery's north wall, come from the tomb of Marie de La Roche, as attested by the dedicatory plaque dated from 1497. This mausoleum, which was originally located in the priory destroyed in 1784, was reassembled in the parish church before being torn down by order of Alexandre Lenoir in order to round out the collections of the Musée des Monuments Français housed in the former Petits-Augustins monastery in Paris. Behind the corridor, the visitor enters a strange succession of three troglodytic chapels designed by the architect Joseph Antoine Froelicher (1790 – 1866) between 1816 and 1819, the date of their consecration. The first, known as the "Chapelle du Caveau" (Vault Chapel), is rectangular. It opens on to the disused family crypt, where the absence of facing reveals the alternate layers of limestone and flint. The chapel itself,

like the other two, features a large regular bond painted on the austerely neoclassical walls and vault, which makes the whole look both sepulchral and monumental.

The second chapel, whose three windows were depicted in the mid-17th century engraving by Israël Silvestre, is at the centre of the layout. It is covered with a

1 Underground staircase
2 Galerie des Chapelles
3 Chapels
4 Reservoir

The Galerie des Chapelles, against the cliff and, to the right, the main staircase wing.

The Galerie des Chapelles, interior.

The Chapelle du Calvaire.

Dovecote staircase, carved out of the rock.

basket-handle♦ vault that ends in a half dome above the altar. Dedicated to the Sacred Heart, it still contains sumptuous terracotta high-reliefs depicting various episodes of the life of Saint Pience. The choice of this iconographic programme is a direct reference to the origins of La Roche-Guyon, where Saint Nicasius converted the "noble lady of the place". The third chapel, known as the "Chapelle du Calvaire" (Calvary Chapel), is home to the tombstone of the Duchess of Enville, as well as a handsome neoclassical altar in coloured breccia.

The dovecote

The corridor leading to the chapels also leads to the troglodytic dovecote, whose existence is attested from the 17th century in the engraving by Israël Silvestre.
This rare example of a dovecote housed in a *bove* features a particularly well-conserved group of 1,500 pigeonholes hollowed out of the limestone.
A large opening edged by a timber-framed parapet affords the visitor a panoramic view of the chateau's rooftops and the valley.

Dovecote staircase, carved out of the rock.

♦Basket-handle (arch):
arch with a surbased curve.

The underground staircase

In the 14th century, the keep built on the edge of the plateau communicated with the main building only via this underground staircase of some 100 steps carved out of the rock, scaling a difference in height of about 40 metres. It comprises two parts: a north-south corridor, whose upper section is behind a double-door chamber that originally opened on to a covered room between the two enceintes of the keep, and the lower section, with an east-west aspect, leading to an edifice that was attached to the main building.

The defenders of the fortress could thus move about unbeknown to potential attackers. Since the cliff was re-cut in 1660, the lower section of the underground staircase has been in the open air and a footbridge supports the steps for about 10 metres. It seems that its construction began from both ends.

The keep

The keep is undoubtedly the best-known element of the chateau since Eugène Viollet-le-Duc's study of it in his *Dictionnaire raisonné de l'architecture française* (Analytical Dictionary of French Architecture, see p. 5). Despite the errors in the analysis of the site, notably the invention of a feudal motte behind the keep, it was the first attempt at recreating the original state of the tower of La Roche-Guyon.

At the end of the first phase of construction, around 1180 – 90, the 40-metre-tall keep dominated the Epte river valley. Trimmed down in 1793, it is now one-third of its original height. A roundheaded door with a monolithic tympanum, typical of Romanesque architecture, commands the entrance located 2 metres from the ground; in the past, it was reached by a removable ladder. This door opened on to a blind lower room, which in turn opened on to a spiral staircase leading to the boarded-over upper room, with its four narrow windows. During a somewhat later

rework, the keep was surrounded by a first rampart from the inside of which emerged the underground staircase leading to the lower chateau. The second enceinte, whose monumental gate was built in the 18th century, completes the tower's defence system.

Across the village

The leaves of its main door comprise twelve panels finely sculpted with arabesques in the early Renaissance style. It houses the tomb of François de Silly, the first duke of La Roche-Guyon, which is by the sculptor Nicolas Guillain († 1639), who, five years earlier, had also executed, at the request of Antoinette de Pons, a funerary monument for herself and her husband Charles du Plessis (church of Liancourt, Oise). The duke is depicted praying, dressed in the cloak of the Ordre du Saint-Esprit, kneeling in front of a cushion upon which rested the statue of an infant in swaddling clothes (stolen in

François de Silly, funerary statue sculpted by François Nicolas Guillain, marble, c. 1630, postcard, c. 1910 (Cg 95 AOA).

The church of Saint-Samson

In 1404 Charles VII authorised the lords of La Roche-Guyon to pull down the old parish church to put up a new building dedicated to Saint Samson outside the enceinte of their chateau. Finished during the second decade of the 16th century, the church has a five-bay nave, framed by rib-vaulted side aisles.

the early 1980s) depicting his only daughter, who died young. The precious altar painting has been attributed to Giuseppe Bartolomeo Chiari.

This *Adoration of the Magi* was given to the parish in 1803 by the Princess of Léon, mother of the future Cardinal of Rohan.

The fountain

From the Middle Ages, La Roche-Guyon's hydraulic network distributed running water to the chateau. Tapped on the plateau of Chérence, the water travelled through 3 kilometres of underground tunnels to a reservoir dug out of the cliff from the 14th century onward. In 1742 Duke Alexandre de La Rochefoucauld, having decided to renovate the chateau's water conveyance, asked Louis De Villars to put up, "for public use", a fountain in the village square. The sculptor Jamay executed the architect's designs. The rockwork amortisement of the fountain, in the early Louis XV style, was recently restored. On a fluted square pedestal with cut-off corners, four volutes frame two basins on opposite sides.

The Armand-Trousseau hospital buildings

The municipality of La Roche-Guyon owes its hospital to the generosity of Count Georges de La Rochefoucauld, who in 1850 begged his father to finance the construction of the first pavilion intended to accommodate convalescent children of the hospitals of Paris. A second phase of works enlarged the establishment in 1854. The hospital then contained 111 beds. The Théodore-Marie Fortin bequest meant that new buildings "in aid of the poor children of the religious schools of Paris" could be built in 1890. After the 1922 departure of the nuns who had been responsible for teaching until then, isolation wards replaced the classrooms. The Pavillon Fortin now accommodates multiply handicapped children. Through its generosity, the La Rochefoucauld family thus revived, after the French Revolution, the age-old philanthropic tradition of the lords of La Roche-Guyon who, from the 11th century, aided the priory of the Sainte-Trinité with their charity. The priory, built on the site of the landscaped garden, fell into disuse from the 17th century and was demolished in 1784.

The town hall-covered market

Inaugurated on 8 May 1847, this novel building combined a covered market with a town hall housed in the upper levels —an example of rationalised architecture by the Conseil des Bâtiments Civils. On the ground floor, seven arches open on to a covered market with seven rows of baseless Doric columns. On the first floor, two wings with roundheaded windows frame a terrace that opens on to the village high street.

The cowshed

(Private property closed to the public.)

The cowshed is thought to date back to the first half of the 18th century. This building housed the octroi officer, collector of the tax levied by the Duke de La Rochefoucauld on Seine traffic. The duke had the exclusive privilege of this toll but in return had to maintain the embankments of the river and secure the transport of men and livestock.

The elegant brick-and-stone main building with five bays and a square upper floor features a light central avant-corps topped by a pediment with lively shapes.

View from the keep.
1 Church of Saint-Samson
2 Town hall-covered market
3 The cowshed

A short bibliography

Baratault, Anne-Claire et al.,
Curiositas humana est: le château de La Roche-Guyon, un salon scientifique au siècle des Lumières (Val d'Oise Éditions, 1998).

Daufresne, Geneviève et al.,
Le château de La Roche-Guyon (Rennes: Ouest-France, 1998).

Dumont-Fillon, Nathalie,
"Les politiques publiques de paysage et de patrimoine, un outil de gestion des territoires: le cas du marais Vernier (Eure) et des coteaux de La Roche-Guyon (Val-d'Oise)", doctoral thesis in environmental science (Paris: École nationale du génie rural, des eaux et forêts, 2002).

Germa, Antoine,
"Les Promenades du château de La Roche-Guyon: étude de l'aménagement d'un parc, 1763-1791", master's thesis (Université Paris XIII, 2002).

Jacobs, Edgar Pierre,
The Time Trap: The Adventures of Blake and Mortimer (Catalan Communications, 1989).

Mesqui, Jean,
Châteaux forts et fortifications de France (Paris: Flammarion, 1997).

Morin, Christophe,
Au service du château (Paris: Publications de la Sorbonne, 2008).

Olivereau, Christian et al.,
Le Retour d'Esther, les fastes retrouvés du château de La Roche-Guyon, exh. cat. (Paris: Créaphis, 2001).

Rouet, Marion,
Étude d'un potager au XVIIIᵉ siècle: l'exemple du château de La Roche-Guyon, master's thesis (Université Paris XIII, 2001).

Rousse, Émile,
La Roche-Guyon, châtelains, château et bourg (Paris: Hachette, 1892). Coll. Monographies des villes et villages de France (Reprint Autremencourt: Lorisse, 2006).

Toupet, Christophe et al.,
"Les réseaux hydrauliques du château de La Roche-Guyon", *Bulletin archéologique du Vexin français* 36 (2004).

Vaugelade, Daniel,
Le Salon physiocratique des La Rochefoucauld (Paris: Publibook, 2001).

Viré, Marc,
Étude d'archéologie architecturale du château de La Roche-Guyon (Val-d'Oise) (Service Départemental d'Archéologie du Val-d'Oise, May – August 1994).

Acknowledgements

François Scellier, president, Conseil Général du Val d'Oise; Raymond Lavaud, president, Établissement Public du Château de La Roche-Guyon and vice-president, Conseil Général Chargé de la Culture, du Tourisme et des Loisirs; Séverine Freyssinier, Armelle Maugin, and Christian Olivereau of the cultural action management team; Jérôme Blachon, Geneviève Daufresne, Jocelyne Le Corre, and Agnès Somers of the Archives Départementales management. Yves Chevallier, director, Château de La Roche-Guyon; Pierre-André Lablaude, chief architect, Monuments Historiques, for authorising the reproduction of his plans.

Captions

AOA: Antiquités et Objets d'Art.
AD 95: Archives Départementales du Val-d'Oise, Cergy-Pontoise.
BNF: Bibliothèque Nationale de France, Paris.
Cg 95 AOA: Conseil Général du Val d'Oise, Antiquités et Objets d'Art, Cergy-Pontoise.
CMN: Centre des Monuments Nationaux, Paris.
MAP/AP: Médiathèque de l'Architecture et du Patrimoine, Archives Photographiques, Paris.
RMN: Réunion des Musées Nationaux, Paris.

Covers
Front cover: the Château de La Roche-Guyon.
Back cover: see p. 43.
Front outer flap: cabinet, Tour Carrée.

Visit
p. 34: slate and shingle roofs overlooking the Cour des Chiens.

Chronology
From left to right and from top to bottom:
• The La Roche family: see pp. 2, 3, 6c, church of Saint-Samson (S. Hitau), siege of 1449, Chronique by Jean Chartier, f. 152, 15th century (BNF, Manuscrits Fr.), see p. 15.
• The Silly family: see pp. 50t, 11t, 68c.
• The Plessis-Liancourt family: see p. 13.
• The La Rochefoucauld family: pp. 12, 17, 46t, 24t, 22bl, 23b.
• The Rohan family: see pp. 24b, 64t.
• The La Rochefoucauld family: see pp. 30, 23–24, 32t.

Photographic credits

Aberdeen Art Gallery: 31t; AD 60: 11b ; AD 95/L. Baude and C. Brossais: 6b, 9t, 12, 14–15, 25b, 33t, 56c, 57b, 58t, 68b; BNF: 2, 3, 6c, 7, 11t, 13, 18, 26, 27; Cg 95 AOA: 25t; AOA/J.-Y. Lacôte: 19t and b, 46t, 53b, 54, 55; Cg 95 AOA/A. Maugin: 30, 31b; CMN/P. Berthé: 22–23t, 28b, 45; C. Donélian: front inner flap; S. Hitau: front cover, 1, 5, 9b, 16, 28, 29, 34–38t, 39b, 40–44, 46b–53t, 56–57t, 58b–68 t and b, 69–71; Musées de la Ville de Rouen/D. Tragin and C. Lancien: 20–21; Free Library of Philadelphia: 8; RMN: 24t; RMN/All rights reserved/ADAGP: 32–33b; RMN/D. Arnaudet: 19c; RMN/G. Blot: 10, 17, 22b; RMN/MAP/AP: 24b, 32t; RMN/T. Le Mage: 4; RMN/R.-G. Ojéda: 39t; RMN/Reversement Kodak: 23b.

Series editor
Alix Sallé
Editorial coordinator
Armelle Bonis
Picture researchers
Joanna Korol, Dalloula Haiouani
Translator
Chrisoula Petridis
Copy editor
Susan Schneider
Graphic design
Atalante/Paris
Graphics
Marc Brugier
Production coordinator
Carine Merse
Photoengraving
SCEI/Ivry-sur-Seine
Printing
Néo-Typo/Besançon, France

© Éditions du patrimoine, Centre des monuments nationaux, Paris, 2008
Dépôt légal : March 2008

ISSN 1159-1722
ISBN 978-2-85822-988-8